WELCOME ·TO
DAILY DEVO1
FOR BOYS 8-12

INTRODUCTION TO THE PARENTS

Hello! Thank you for purchasing this book. My name is Randell Holmes, the author of this book. I want to share my vision with you behind this book...

I believe the earlier you can teach a child about the Word of God, the better. If a child is raised properly knowing the truth of God, then he or she could save themselves from a lot of painful mistakes if they did not know the Bible. The truth is that at a young age, we believe almost everything we hear and see. There is both good and bad that come from this. Obviously, the bad is the first that comes to mind. But we have an opportunity to truly use this for good. Since children are so susceptive about believing anything, let's feed these children the ACTUAL truth and something that is worth believing. For it says in Romans 8:5, "For those who live according to the flesh set their minds on the things of the flesh, but those who live according to the Spirit set their minds on the things of the Spirit." If we can pour into these boys at a young age and fill their minds with things of the Spirit, it will be a part of them as they grow older and will encourage them to be men of God.

DAY 1

"I CHOSE YOU." – JOHN 15:16

Daily Devotional: It is important that you know you are destined to do great things for God because he chose you for it. As Jesus chose his disciples, he chose you too to follow him and live for him. You got saved because he called you and reached out to you. He chose you first before you chose to go with him.

This applies to every Christian, and it's a great privilege/benefit from God to us. See it this way: The great being in the universe chose to come to you and change your life for good. He gave you purpose, a meaning to life, and then gave his word to guide you according to that purpose.

Although there are still many out there that aren't saved, he chose them too, and he is only waiting patiently for the time they will hear him calling. So pray for them as you should.

Daily Do: Say this prayer "God, I know you chose me according to your purpose, and I am grateful for this honor. Help me to fulfill all that you have chosen me for in Jesus' name" Amen.

DAY 2

TRAIN UP A CHILD IN THE WAY HE SHOULD GO; EVEN WHEN HE IS OLD, HE WILL NOT DEPART FROM IT." – PROVERBS 22:6

Daily Devotional: Many times, mom and dad tell you what to do. Every adult that cares about you will always do that. Do you know why? They are training you on the right path that God wants for you. God has commanded them in the Bible to teach you the right things and help you get better with the gifts and abilities you have, so you can become the great man God sees in you. The more you obey mom and dad, the more God will be happy with you.

You do not know what is best for you, but mom and dad do because God has shown them. So, you must learn to trust God and your parents.

Someday soon, you will be a grown man, and all that mom and dad have taught you now as a kid will help you in your future. You will always remember their words, and you will make godly choices in all that you do because you listened to them.

Daily Do: God's commandment says, "Children, obey your parents in the Lord, for this is right." So, obey God's word by listening to your mom and dad and doing exactly what they tell you to do. No more disobedience, okay? You can do this!

DAY 3

"TREAT PEOPLE IN THE SAME WAY THAT YOU WANT THEM TO TREAT YOU." – LUKE 6:31

Daily Devotional: Our Lord Jesus commanded us to be kind to others if we want them to be kind to us. Think of the time someone did something nice for you – it felt really good right? Now think again of something mean someone once did to you – you definitely don't want to experience such again. Jesus knows this; that's why he wants his children to be kind to one another.

There is a story of two boys who lived close to each another; one was named John, and the other was Willis. One day, John's parents bought him some candies and asked him to share them with Willis, but John refused to share. He had so many but still left Willis with nothing. Willis had his birthday a few days later, and John wasn't invited. He felt sad that all the kids in the neighborhood were at the party except him. A few moments later, Willis knocked at John's door, and to John's surprise, Willis handed a pack of candy to John, then asked him to join the party. John felt so sorry for not being nice to Willis days ago, but Willis smiled and replied "My parents taught me to be nice to people if I want them to be nice to me". Now you can see that Willis did not wait for John to be nice before he acted kindly to him. He did not repay evil for evil; instead, he acted as Jesus would.

Daily Do: From this moment forward, do something nice for people you meet, even when they don't do the same to you. Your act of kindness will change their hearts, and God will move unexpected people to show kindness to you. As the bible also says "You will reap what you sow".

DAY 4

"JESUS CHRIST IS THE SAME YESTERDAY, TODAY, AND FOREVER." – HEBREWS 13:8

Daily Devotional: God is an unchanging God, which means Jesus is an unchanging Jesus. The same person he was years ago is the same person he is today, and the same forever. You read in your Bible that he healed the sick and showed love to sinners and the poor; He still does the same today and will continue to do so. All the commandments and teachings he gave still apply to us today. That is, he never changed what he says is good for us and what isn't good for us. If he never tolerated stealing, killing, and lying in the Bible, he still doesn't. People try to change the rules when God hasn't, and they end up displeasing God and exposing themselves to the control of the devil.
He said he will never leave you nor forsake you, he said he will protect you and bless you. Those promises last forever because he lasts forever. You are therefore in safe hands.

Let the words of Jesus guide you today, tomorrow, and forever. Never join those who break or change the words of Jesus to please themselves. Stay blessed!

Daily Do: Stick to one and only Jesus for the rest of your life, and stay away from sinful activities.

DAY 5

NO ONE CAN SERVE TWO MASTERS."
– MATTHEW 6:24

Daily Devotional: Here, Jesus taught his disciples that "no one can serve two masters; he will either hate one and love the other or be loyal to one and despise the other". Then he added, "You cannot serve God and mammon". Mammon means physical things. But it could also mean anything that takes the place of God in a man's heart. The Israelites in ancient times once thought they could serve God and an Idol called Baal. But in the sight of God, it is an act of betrayal and rebellion to serve an Idol and serve him too because human hearts cannot be loyal to two masters. This is not the same as having two jobs, one at a coffee shop and a dog shelter. This form of service has to do with the heart, the ownership of life; you either surrender your life to God and serve him, or you surrender and serve another spirit or idol, which is a sin. Men and women are all created by God, and their lives should be a total service to their creator because we belong to him; not the enemy or another physical thing.

Belonging to God means belonging to everything he stands for – holiness, righteousness, faith, joy, peace, mercy, kindness, gentleness, etc. Some people claim to be Christians, but when they want something so bad, they go to the devil to get it instead of waiting for God to give them. This means their hearts don't belong to God. Being a Christian is not about the title but your lifestyle. Don't be so desperate to have a lot of money that you are willing to do just about anything to get it.

Daily Do: Ask yourself, "Who do I belong to?" Let your heart and desires be directed only towards God and nothing else.

DAY 6

"SET YOUR MINDS ON THINGS ABOVE, NOT EARTHLY THINGS." – COLOSSIANS 3:2

Daily Devotional: Believers are to fix their minds on heaven while they live here on earth. The things on earth are temporal; that is they do not last forever. Whereas the things in heaven are eternal, they last forever and ever. Our real home as God's children is in heaven, so we must not be carried away by the things we see and own on earth because on the day a man dies, he loses all his earthly possessions, he can't take his clothes, shoes, and car to heaven, can he?

So, the scripture above teaches us to seek heavenly things above earthly things. This is important because the devil has successfully tried to replace God with earthly materials in people's hearts. That is why many people prefer money and fame over salvation and a relationship with God. You must never fall into this trap of the enemy. Let your desire be channeled towards God, Jesus, and the Holy Spirit. The more you study your Bible, the more you fix your heart and mind on heaven and pleasing God. Keep in mind that you need some earthly things like money, education, jobs, clothes, and shoes, to live well on earth, God wants that for you, but when these earthly things begin to replace God in your heart, it becomes a sin.

Daily Do: Always remember that you are like a man traveling through the earth, and you must represent Christ all your days. Do not get distracted by the worldly things around you. Heaven is the goal, earth is the journey.

DAY 7

"BEFORE I FORMED YOU IN THE WOMB, I KNEW YOU." — JEREMIAH 1:5

Daily Devotion: You were once so little like a seed in your mom's womb. You were kept safe in there until your birth. God says he already knew you before that even happened. Isn't that incredible? You were in heaven with him before he sent you as a gift to your parents. You definitely can't remember that, but God did know you.

God already chose your name and who he wants you to become, even before your mom and dad ever knew you. This means you are so precious to God, you have always belonged with him, and it should stay that way here on earth.

Daily Do: Say this prayer to God "Thank you Lord for creating me in your image; thank you for the plans you have for me; help me to live for you all my days on earth" Amen.

DAY 8

"SO DO NOT FEAR, FOR I AM WITH YOU; DO NOT BE [SCARED], FOR I AM YOUR GOD. I WILL STRENGTHEN YOU AND HELP YOU; I WILL UPHOLD YOU WITH MY RIGHTEOUS RIGHT HAND." – ISAIAH 41:10

Daily Devotion: Have you ever been in a dark place and you can't help but be afraid? Your mind suddenly switches to a fearful mode, and you begin to think that a monster or something else you saw in a movie will creep out. This is not God's will for you as his child. The scripture above is a direct command and promise from God. He said this to the Israelites, and he is also saying it to you right now – Do not fear anything, for God is with you. Check out 2 Timothy 1:7. It says that the Lord has not given you the spirit of fear, but of power, and of love, and of a sound mind. Now, that is God's will for you. You have the power and love of God in you, and you have a sound mind. The devil wants to take that away from you by making you afraid – do not allow him.

God has promised to give you strength and help you in every good thing you do. He will help you do better in school, sports practice, music class, drawing class, and more. Just take a moment to imagine his huge powerful hand holding your little hand. You are safe forever!

Daily Do: Repeat the words "I _____(say your name), will not fear, for God is with me; I will not be scared for he is my God. He will strengthen me and help me; he will hold me with his mighty hand".

DAY 9

"DO ALL THINGS WITHOUT COMPLAINING AND ARGUING." – PHILIPPIANS 2:14

Daily Devotion: Have you ever complained when something doesn't go the way you want? You probably cried, yelled, or refused to do what you were told. As a child of God, you are expected to stay calm, and grateful in all that you do. Do not argue with your parents or friends. Learn to listen more than you speak. God wants you to be at peace with everyone, no matter what they do to you – you become more like Jesus when you do that. Also, when someone says something false about you, do not do the same to them, be a better example, and show a little Jesus in your world.

When you pray, God wants to hear your grateful words, not complaints about what he has not done yet. A lot of people do this when they pray, and it displeases God.

So, the scripture above commands you not to grumble in your conversation with God, your parents, teachers, coaches, and friends, especially because you feel unhappy and unsatisfied about something.

Daily Do: Get a diary and write down the things you are grateful for. Also, decide that you will not complain or argue with anyone through this week and forward.

DAY 10

"FOR WE ARE HIS WORKMANSHIP, CREATED IN CHRIST JESUS FOR GOOD WORKS, WHICH GOD PREPARED BEFOREHAND THAT WE SHOULD WALK IN THEM." – EPHESIANS 2:10

Daily Devotion: A potter molds clay into a shape he already has in his mind. He keeps on shaping it until it is perfect. God is also a potter, and you are his clay. He longs to mold you into the shape he desires. And I don't mean the size of your body, but your mind, your life, and your destiny. Your destiny is what God has planned for you to become in life. God didn't save you just so you can go to heaven, but he wants to make something beautiful out of you. The word "workmanship" in the scripture above, means "work of art", just like the drawings or paintings you make. In the Greek language, it means we are God's beautiful artwork. That is just so lovely to hear, right? You are a masterpiece that God is carefully composing. He is surely a great artist, so your life will come out beautiful.

God wants to take you where you are right now to where he desires for you to be. Let him work on you so you can do good works for his kingdom throughout your lifetime.

Daily Do: Pray to God now and say "Thank you Lord for saving me; I submit to your workings in my life, mold me and make me into what you desire." Amen.

DAY 11

"BUT WHY DO YOU JUDGE YOUR BROTHER? OR WHY DO YOU SHOW CONTEMPT FOR YOUR BROTHER? FOR WE SHALL ALL STAND BEFORE THE JUDGMENT SEAT OF CHRIST." – ROMANS 14:10

Daily Devotional: As a child of God, you are not to judge a fellow Christian just because they are not doing some things the way you do them. They are still God's creation just like you; and if they sin, pray for them, don't shut them out. As Christians, we are all God's children – we are a family. So, as a true family of Christ, God wants us to love, support, and respect each other. We all have our differences because we are different people with unique minds and attitudes. Imagine if there was only one color in the world, will that be any fun? No! There wouldn't be a beautiful rainbow, clothes, cars, paints, and shoes of various colors. In fact, the earth wouldn't look beautiful and alive. That is why God is the greatest artist for coming up with so many colors to decorate the earth.

Therefore, if colors are fun and unique, so are humans. The world would be boring if every person were the same. So the point is, to respect other Christians and embrace them even when there are things you do not have in common. Choose to focus on what you have in common, which is JESUS CHRIST.

*Note that we are not to judge non-Christians because they are already judged by God in the Bible; they do not have eternal life until they accept Jesus into their hearts. Pray for them to be saved and speak to them about the love of Jesus.

Daily Do: Appreciate everyone in your life for being different. That's what brings beauty into our world.

DAY 12

"FOR EVERYONE WHO CALLS ON THE NAME OF THE LORD WILL BE SAVED." – ROMANS 10:13

Daily Devotion: I have constantly called you a child of God since the first day you began studying this devotional. Today, I would love to ask you a question: are you saved? This simply means, have you surrendered your life to Jesus and chosen to make him your Lord and Savior? You do this simply by calling upon his name, letting go of your sins, and believing in him. Romans 10:9-10 has two major keywords – confess and believe. "If you confess with your mouth the Lord Jesus and believe in your heart that God raised him from the dead, you will be saved. For with the heart, one believes unto righteousness, and with the mouth, confession is made unto salvation."

So, I'll ask again: are you saved? Make sure you do this right because the Bible tells us it's important. Being saved sets you free from the power of sin – you become a true-born child of God.

Daily Do: You must be wondering how to do all I said above. Well, it will be an honor to guide you. Pray this out loud with all your heart: "Lord Jesus, I believe you died on the cross for me to be saved from sin and death. Forgive me of all my sins. I confess that you alone are God, and I accept you into my life today, to become my Lord and Savior. I love you, Lord. Thank you for saving me. Amen."
Congratulations, if you prayed those prayers. Heaven rejoices over you right now!

DAY 13

"DON'T BE DEFEATED BY EVIL, BUT DEFEAT EVIL WITH GOOD." – ROMANS 12:21

Daily Devotion: When Jesus was treated badly; beaten, spat on, mocked, laughed at, and nailed to the cross, it only makes sense for him to defend himself by calling down mighty angels to avenge him, right? He is God anyway, he does have the power to defeat those wicked men, but he didn't. He chose not to repay evil for evil; instead, he repaid evil for good. That is, he gave them grace and love in return for the evil done to him.

We are commanded to love our enemies and be kind-hearted to those who aren't kind to us. That was what God – the Father – did for us. He chose for his son Jesus to die for us while we were yet sinners. He did something so awesome for us even when we did not deserve it. When you repay someone with evil, you drag yourself down to their level; you become as bad as them. And God does not want that.
So, choose to love, choose to be nice, and say kind words to people. Dare to be different, just like Jesus was.

Daily Do: Is there someone you know that isn't nice to you? Say a warm 'hello' to them this week, give them a small gift, and tell them that Jesus loves them. Don't worry about their reply or reaction. Make Jesus proud!

DAY 14

"GOD SAVED YOU BY HIS GRACE WHEN YOU BELIEVED. AND YOU CAN'T TAKE CREDIT FOR THIS; IT IS A GIFT FROM GOD." – EPHESIANS 2:8

Daily Devotion: Imagine there was a 16-year-old boy named Luke. One day Luke was speeding and got pulled over by a cop. The cop issued Luke a ticket for $300. Luke does not have a job and cannot pay for the ticket and therefore has to go to court. A few days later, Luke goes to court to attempt to settle the conflict. The conflict being that Luke owes $300 that he does not have. When Luke enters the courtroom, he sees that the judge is his dad. Luke knew his father was a judge but did not expect him to be the judge of his case. Luke tells his father that he knows what he did was wrong. He went over the speed limit which is against the law, but he does not have the money to pay the punishment. Rather than sending his own son to jail, the judge said, "Luke, my son, I know you cannot pay this debt. But because I love you and because I want to show mercy I will cleanse you of your debt. You no longer owe $300. However even though I am a merciful judge, I am also a fair and just judge. This is why the $300 cannot just go unpaid. Someone has to pay the consequence of your actions. As a result, I will pay for your ticket. I will take the debt that you deserve."

This is very similar to how God loves and shows mercy to us. We are in debt to Jesus. We have all sinned and according to Romans 6:23, "The wages of sin is death." The punishment of sin is separation from Christ, but since he loves you so dearly, he cleanses you of your debt. Jesus did this by living a perfect life and dying on the cross so that you and I do not have to. That is grace. That is true love.

Daily Do: Tell Jesus how thankful you are for what he did for you.

DAY 15

"INSTEAD OF EACH PERSON WATCHING OUT FOR THEIR OWN GOOD, WATCH OUT FOR WHAT IS BETTER FOR OTHERS." – PHILIPPIANS 2:4

Daily Devotion: Being selfless is one of the most important characteristics of a Christian. Jesus showed this when he died on the cross. He did not consider or think about what was good for him, but he chose to do what was best for us.

The scripture above is talking about the fact that there would be no troubles among people – especially Christians – when they are selfless with one another. Humility is the key to living this kind of life. That is, you must be a humble person – someone who is not arrogant, but meek like Jesus. Worldly kings are known for being prideful. Worldly kings expect to be served, yet Jesus the King of Kings came to serve others. Jesus humbled himself to take on the form of a servant. That's incredible.

Learn to look out for others, even while you look out for yourself. Don't be selfish, caring only for YOU. Live a Godly life today by placing the needs of someone above yours. Remember, this does not mean you should not care for yourself but show the same care for others every time you get the chance.

Daily Do: Decide to put someone's needs before yours this week. It could be your brother, sister, parents, or friend. Continue this and watch God honor you by meeting your needs.

DAY 16

"THUS SAYS THE LORD TO YOU, 'DO NOT BE AFRAID AND DO NOT BE DISMAYED AT THIS GREAT [TROUBLE], FOR THE BATTLE IS NOT YOURS BUT GOD'S." – 2 CHRONICLES 20:15

Daily Devotional: When the Israelites were confronted by their enemies, it seemed like they were about to lose the fight since they were outnumbered (Their enemies were more in number than them). Suddenly, the Spirit of God came upon a young man among them named Jahaziel. And he said, "Thus says the Lord, 'do not be afraid and do not be dismayed at this great trouble, for the battle is not yours but God's". This gave peace and confidence to the people of God, and they were assured that God will fight the battle for them as he had said.

Imagine a bully trying to beat up a kid, and the Lord tells the kid not to be afraid because the fight belongs to God, not the boy. This means that God is committed to defending and standing up for the boy more than his parents or teachers ever could.

Everything standing as a bully or enemy in your life will also bow to the God who stands by you. No one can defeat God so no one can defeat you either. Your fight is his fight. Hallelujah!

Daily Do: Say this prayer "Thank you Lord for being my defender. I am grateful that I am never alone in any battle I face in life, for you are with me. In Jesus' name, I pray" Amen.

DAY 17

"DO NOTHING OUT OF SELFISH AMBITION OR VAIN CONCEIT. RATHER, IN HUMILITY VALUE OTHERS ABOVE YOURSELVES." – PHILIPPIANS 2:3

Daily Devotional: As you have previously learned before today, Jesus lived a selfless life when he was on earth – he placed the interests of others before his. Living a selfless life might seem unfair or even hard sometimes. But remember, doing good things is not always easy. As humans, there is a part of us that prefers what God hates, and it just wants to do whatever it likes without any control. That part is called FLESH. You see, we must never give in to our flesh at any time; that way it dies gradually and loses its control. If you submit to the spirit of God to help you stay humble and serve others, your flesh dies. This is not something you do once, but DAILY. Your flesh will take any chance it gets to make you act selfishly, but you have the power of God in you to say NO.

Daily Do: Walk in the spirit and not in the flesh, by doing what God tells you every day.

DAY 18

"GIVE THANKS TO THE LORD, FOR HE IS GOOD; HIS LOVE ENDURES FOREVER." – PSALM 107:1

Daily Devotional: Thanksgiving is an act that attracts God to men. We give thanks to God when we pray, sing praises, and worship. Imagine your mom or dad got you a Christmas gift, and you loved it, but never said a simple "Thank you". You will only discourage them from doing even more for you. When you are grateful for something, you get so much more of it, sooner or later. Saying "Thank you" to God shows that you acknowledge how good he's been to you – he has shown you his love, mercy, and grace.

God deserves your thanksgiving. He has been with you all your life, and he will do anything for you to stay safe in his arms.

Daily Do: Give thanks to God for being good to you and showing you his mercies daily. Thank him also for everyone and everything you have.

DAY 19

"LET ALL THAT YOU DO BE DONE WITH LOVE."
– 1 CORINTHIANS 16:14

Daily Devotional: Let Love guide you in all you do. When you speak, think, play, learn, and do any other activity, live as though God is walking with you every second, because he is.

If there are any words or thoughts that displease him, let go of them immediately. God wants your dear heart to stay pure and holy. Through love, your heart becomes more like God's every time. Do not allow hate into your heart; never say you hate someone, no matter what they do wrong.

Daily Do: Have you told someone you love them today? If not, do so.

DAY 20

Daily Devotional: I have a friend named Preston who once passed by a coffee shop and saw a young boy sitting outside. Preston would go by this coffee shop daily and see the young boy; the young boy always looked sad, gloomy, and lonely. Preston wanted to ask him what was bothering his mind, but could not soak up the courage to talk to him. So, one day Preston prayed to God to give him the boldness to step out of his comfort zone. Later that same day, Preston ran into the young boy and asked him if he was ok. The young boy shared sad things going on in his life, and how he had no one to live with. From this conversation, Preston felt God calling him to legally adopt the young boy and give him a better experience in life. So Preston did so, and now the is 12 years old, and thriving at church and in school.

The lesson I want you to learn from this is to notice those moments God gives you to check on someone, help them out on something, or even listen to them. All that many need is a shoulder to cry on, a warm hug, a listening ear, and sometimes food, water, and money. You don't have to do what is beyond you; that is something you can't afford to give. The little things you can offer are more than enough, and they can change a life.

Daily Do: If you ever have the opportunity to help anyone, don't hesitate, do it with all your heart. Do an act of kindness and help someone out today.

DAY 21

"LET'S NOT GET TIRED OF DOING GOOD, BECAUSE IN TIME WE'LL HAVE A HARVEST IF WE DON'T GIVE UP." – GALATIANS 6:9

Daily Devotional: Have you ever tried planting before? When a farmer sows orange seeds into the ground, he waters it daily and expects it to grow into a tree and bear many oranges. But that does not happen in one day, or two, or three. It requires patience to reap the harvest of whatever a person sows; it could take weeks, months, and even years.

In the same way, when you do good things, you are sowing seeds, and you will reap your fruits when the time for harvest comes – the time your good works grow into huge trees. God's message to you today is that you must not give up or get tired of being a good boy – do not get sick of being kind to unkind people. You have probably done something good for someone, and it looks like nothing good is happening in return for you. Wait patiently; you will surely receive your fruits in multiple folds. God is making sure of it.

Daily Do: Say this prayer "Lord Jesus, I believe you reward those that do good things in your name. Help me to plant good seeds in life and reap my harvest in due time" Amen.

DAY 22

**FOR THE THINGS WHICH ARE SEEN ARE TEMPORARY, BUT THE THINGS WHICH ARE NOT SEEN ARE ETERNAL."
– 2 CORINTHIANS 4:18**

Daily Devotional: The things which are seen are the experiences we go through in life, especially the challenges and problems. While the things we do not see are waiting in heaven, and we will get from God after leaving this world. There is glory ahead of us – peace, joy, love, fulfillment, and every good thing beyond our imaginations. Do not be distracted or disturbed by the problems you face in life right now as a child, and even when you become an adult.

The older you get, the greater challenges you will face, but do not worry; you will keep growing strong enough to handle them all because you know now that your problems in life do not last forever – every problem has an expiry date. God has a great reward for you; keep running, keep trying, keep gaining strength; you have the victory in Christ Jesus.

Daily Do: Say this scripture out loud "The Lord is my refuge and my strength; a very present help in trouble".

DAY 23

"CHILDREN ARE A GIFT FROM THE LORD; THEY ARE A REWARD FROM HIM." – PSALM 127:3

Daily Devotional: Every child is a gift from God to their parents and the world. A family is only really complete with a child in it, and that's because children bring joy, happiness, and fulfillment to a home. Adults are more protective when they have children because children cannot protect themselves, nor can they provide what they need. When God gives people children, he expects them to care for those kids until they become adults.

Parents are responsible for how their kids turn out in their adulthood, because God gave those children to them, and they are commanded to teach their kids in the way of the Lord – to honor and fear God in all they do. Sadly, many kids are left to themselves to do whatever they want; this was never God's plan. Children are lovely rewards from God, and they should be treated with all care and patience; they should be fed, protected, and educated.

Daily Do: You are a gift and a blessing from God. Take a minute to pray for kids out there that are not treated as the gifts they truly are. Ask God to protect them and give them caring parents.

DAY 24

"IF GOD IS FOR US, WHO CAN BE AGAINST US?"
– ROMANS 8:31

Daily Devotional: God is for us if we are reconciled to him through Christ Jesus; that means we are on his good side because we believe in Jesus. God is the Almighty and most powerful being ever; no man or devil can defeat him. When God is for you, no one can be against you; no one can defeat you because God's power is working for you; he is on your side. So, it does not matter if someone does not like you; God likes you, and he backs you up when you do the right thing. He will not let harm come your way, because he is your shield and cover; he is greater than any superhero you know. You are undefeatable and unconquerable!

Daily Do: Say this out loud "God is on my side; I shall not fear what man or the devil can do to me. I am untouchable for evil because I have the victory in Christ Jesus".

DAY 25

"FOR GOD SO LOVED THE WORLD, THAT HE GAVE HIS ONLY SON, THAT WHOEVER BELIEVES IN HIM SHOULD NOT PERISH BUT HAVE EVERLASTING LIFE."
– JOHN 3:16

Daily Devotional: God sent his son Jesus Christ to die for us, saving us from sin and spiritual death. This means that we no longer have to do bad things that God hates because Jesus has given us the power to say no to those things, and we are sure to be with God in heaven. Through the sacrifice Jesus made on the cross for humans, we can freely have a relationship with God, by calling him 'Abba' which means Father. When you believe in Jesus and invite him to be the Lord of your life, he will forgive all your wrongs and give you eternal life. This kind of life is called 'Zoe' – it is the life of God that makes you live forever in heaven.

God made this possible because he loves the whole world. He loves you, your family, your friends, your teachers, and everyone else you can think about. He does not want anyone to go to hell, because he wants them in heaven with him as his children. Jesus is the expression of God's love for us.

Daily Do: As God showered his love on you by sending his son Jesus, he expects you to do the same by giving up something precious to you and handing it over to someone else because you love them.

DAY 26

"YOUR WORD IS A LAMP TO MY FEET AND A LIGHT TO MY PATH." – PSALM 119:105

Daily Devotional: Do you love walking? Maybe you do, or maybe you don't. But as long as you have good legs, you will walk; whether to get something in the fridge, to your classroom or to play outside.

It's the same in life, everyone walks; some are slow, while some are fast; some are walking with the Lord, while others aren't. The Bible verse above tells us that the word of God is a lamp to our feet and a light to our path while we walk through life. The word of God is like light bulbs tied to your feet, shining bright lights on the dark road, which is life. Without these light bulbs, you will be in total darkness, not knowing where to go or what to do. God does not want that for you or anyone, which is the reason he sent his word to us. Through his word, we know right from wrong; we also stay on a safe path, avoiding ditches that lead to destruction.

Daily Do: Use the word of God in any situation you find yourself in. Particularly study and memorize Psalm 23, Psalm 121, and Psalm 91. It will always come in handy.

DAY 27

"JESUS SAID, 'LET THE LITTLE CHILDREN COME TO ME, AND DO NOT HINDER THEM, FOR THE KINGDOM OF HEAVEN BELONGS TO SUCH AS THESE."
– MATTHEW 19:14

Daily Devotional: Children are so precious to Jesus. He was a great friend to them while he was on earth, he would lay his hand on their heads and bless them, and he still wants more children to come to him even now. He wants you to come to him; He wants to be your best friend.

He said, "...for the kingdom of heaven belongs to such as these". This means that anyone who wants to go to heaven must be like a child. Kids easily believe what they are told – if your dad promised to get you a gift, you will believe him, right? You might stay awake all night imagining what the gift would be. It never occurs to you that he could fail to keep his promise; you are just excited to get the gift. That is the same faith God wants from all his children, both kids, and adults. Without faith, no one can please God. Keep trusting him for everything you need.

Daily Do: Keep your faith in God; he always listens to you. Also, tell the Lord you are ready to be his friend.

DAY 28

"FOR THE SPIRIT GOD GAVE US DOES NOT MAKE US TIMID, BUT GIVES US POWER, LOVE, AND SELF-DISCIPLINE." – 2 TIMOTHY 1:7

Daily Devotional: Fear is a terrible weapon in the hand of the devil. He wants you to be afraid of everything, whereas God has created you to be as bold as a lion. The spirit of God dwells in you, and he does not make you fear, shy, or timid; instead, he gives you power, love, and self-discipline, which is also "a sound mind" according to the Old King James Bible. Any thought that makes you feel less than someone else is not from God but from the enemy.

Your mental health is protected through the spirit of God because he helps you see yourself the way God sees you; he also makes you positively view life. You are not one of those that give up in the face of challenges; you are a powerful child of God that takes down every mountain or problem that comes your way. Now go and win!

Daily Do: Write own this scripture in your journal, and confess it over your life daily "For God has not given me the spirit of fear, but of power, of love, and a sound mind". Stay bold as a lion!

DAY 29

"THEREFORE, IF ANYONE IS IN CHRIST, HE IS A NEW CREATION." – 2 CORINTHIANS 5:17

Daily Devotional: Anyone who has given his life to Jesus – that is born again – shall be made into a new creation; He/she shall be washed clean from every sin and guilt.

You become like a new baby in the sight of God when he redeems your soul from sin and death. It might sound impossible, but that is exactly what happens spiritually. As a human, you have a spirit inside of you, and that is the real YOU. That is the part of you that gets born again and becomes a new creation in Christ Jesus. After you are made new, you begin to grow daily when you study the word of God – his word is the food you take that helps your spirit becomes strong and energized. Just as you eat daily to stay alive and healthy, you must also eat the word of God by studying and thinking about it daily. Your nature and behavior change to that of Christ when you do this.

Finally, no matter how bad a person may be, God can turn them into new creations if they come to Christ and receive him. He is ready to give everyone a whole new life.

Daily Do: Say this prayer "Thank you Lord for saving my soul and making me a new creation" Amen.

DAY 30

"DO NOT LET ANY UNWHOLESOME TALK COME OUT OF YOUR MOUTHS, BUT ONLY WHAT IS HELPFUL FOR BUILDING OTHERS UP ACCORDING TO THEIR NEEDS, THAT IT MAY BENEFIT THOSE WHO LISTEN."
– EPHESIANS 4:29

Daily Devotion: What kind of words do you speak daily? Do you curse others when you are angry and frustrated? Do you repeat the bad words you hear someone say at school or on TV?

The Bible teaches that Christians should not speak bad words to one another, and even to other people. Your conversation must glorify God; He must be pleased with your words because your words are also your actions. You know, words are powerful weapons; good words warm the heart, while bad words cut and sting. I believe you don't wish to hurt or tear anyone down, right? So speak good words to warm the hearts of people, and even yours.

Build up other people with your words, by telling them things like "Jesus loves you", "You are forgiven", "I love you", "You are amazing", "You look good", and so many more that will bring smiles to their faces. When you do this, many will come to Jesus because they see his nature and character in you.

Daily Do: Speak Godly and positive words to your family, friends, neighbors, teachers, and every other person you come across daily.

DAY 31

"THEREFORE, MY BELOVED, FLEE FROM IDOLATRY."
– 1 CORINTHIANS 10:14

Daily Devotion: The Apostle Paul in his letter to the Corinthian church, tells them to flee from idolatry. But, what exactly is idolatry? It is simply the worship of something or someone other than God. If you love a person so much that you are obsessed with them and God is in second place after that person in your heart, the person has become an idol you worship, and this hurts God's heart.

God must be the first in your heart above everything and anyone else because he is your creator, he owns you, and he loves you more than anyone else could. No one should take his place in your life. People who worship images they call their 'gods' are called idolaters according to the Bible because they are worshipping another god other than the living God that created the heavens and the earth. Do not be an idolater.

Daily Do: Do a clean check of your heart today; is there something or someone that is becoming an idol to you?

DAY 32

"I HAVE NO GREATER JOY THAN TO HEAR THAT MY CHILDREN ARE WALKING IN THE TRUTH." – 3 JOHN 1:4

Daily Devotion: Walking in the truth means living your life according to the truth of God's word. It is important to live as the child of God that you truly are; live your life like everything that belongs to Jesus also belongs to you.

You are not alone, and you are not in charge of your life because God is with you every step of the way. So, do not live your life like an ordinary person who is trying to figure out life on his own.

Have you seen a manual before? It's that book that comes in the box with a TV, video game player, refrigerator, or any new gadget you purchase. This manual gives a guideline on how to use a specific gadget the way the manufacturer intends for you to use it. If you do not do as it says, chances are that you may mess up what you bought.

It's the same way the Bible was written as your manual for living successfully on the earth. There is no other option, you have to follow it to make it in life.

Daily Do: Choose to study your Bible daily and live by the truth that it says.

DAY 33

Daily Devotion: Every living thing in heaven and the earth praises God, except that some humans don't, which is why the scripture above specifically says that everything that has breath should praise the Lord – humans are the only ones that still need a reminder of such. Do you know that even the rocks, sea, and mountains praise the Lord? If these things can sing praises to God, how much more those he created in his image? He created you to look just like him, and he breathe his air into your nostrils to give you life. Therefore he deserves to be praised daily by you. Sing joyful songs to the Lord, shout out his praises, and dance for joy. The Bible instructed this several times in the book of Psalms. Praise is truly a powerful weapon that moves the heart of God toward a man.

Daily Do: Sometime today sing at least one song to God. This can be on the car radio, your headphones, or just aloud. It will bring a heavenly atmosphere around you.

3

DAY 34

**"JESUS REPLIED: 'LOVE THE LORD YOUR GOD WITH ALL YOUR HEART AND WITH ALL YOUR SOUL AND WITH ALL YOUR MIND. THIS IS THE FIRST AND GREATEST COMMANDMENT. AND THE SECOND IS LIKE IT: 'LOVE YOUR NEIGHBOR AS YOURSELF."
– MATTHEW 22:37-38**

Daily Devotion: Jesus teaches us that there are two commandments from God that is the foundation of other commandments. These two commandments are the greatest, and out of them come the other commandments such as, do not steal, do not kill, do not covet, and so on.

Why would these two be the greatest commandments? Well, if you love God with all your heart, soul, and mind, it would be difficult for you to disobey him or displease him. When you love someone, you will do your best to honor that person and bring a smile to their face. Also, when you love people the way you love yourself, you would treat them in a way that you would want to be treated.

Daily Do: Let these two commandments be in your heart always. Also, don't just pray to God, but seek to fall in love with him and build a true relationship with him.

DAY 35

"EVERY WORD OF GOD PROVES TRUE; HE IS A SHIELD TO THOSE WHO TAKE REFUGE IN HIM."
– PROVERBS 30:5

Daily Devotion: Why is the word of God good enough to guide the lives of every human? Why is it the best foundation for us to stand upon?

The scripture above tells us that the word of God is true; it is not mixed with lies or deception, it cannot mislead anyone, except if they misinterpret it. The word of God is pure and holy; his promises are true, and they never fail. God's word is a shield to those who believe and speak it.

God created the heavens and the earth by his word. He said "let there be light," and there was light. He continued to speak until all things were fully formed. If his word is that powerful, then we all need his word to bring light and a total transformation in our lives.

Daily Do: Study the first chapter of the book of Genesis, and trust in God's word to be a covering around your life.

DAY 36

"DON'T LET ANYONE LOOK DOWN ON YOU BECAUSE YOU ARE YOUNG, BUT SET AN EXAMPLE FOR THE BELIEVERS IN SPEECH, IN CONDUCT, IN LOVE, IN FAITH, AND IN PURITY." – 1 TIMOTHY 4:12

Daily Devotion: People can look down on you because you are just a kid, but God sees more than that in you; he sees a great man who will fulfill his purpose on the earth; he sees a mighty man that will bring down the kingdom of darkness. You are more than a kid, you are a follower of Christ who is expected to set an example for others. How do you set a good example as a follower of Christ/Christian? The answer is simple – by living as Christ lived. Are your speech and actions pleasing to God and men? You should study more about Jesus and see how loving, peaceful, kind, gentle, and forgiving he was.

Let people see you and say "oh, I want to be like Josh" – you can replace Josh with your name. People should see Jesus when they look at you; they should look up to you and desire to know God because of you. So, think deeply about this. Are other kids becoming better in life because of you, or are they getting more disrespectful and rebellious? You are not too young to influence other kids positively, and Jesus is counting on you!

Daily Do: Pray to the Lord to help you be a good example to others from today.

DAY 37

**"THEREFORE, WHETHER YOU EAT OR DRINK, OR WHATEVER YOU DO, DO ALL TO THE GLORY OF GOD."
– 1 CORINTHIANS 10:31**

Daily Devotion: In all that you do, remember that God must be glorified. Even the food you eat and the things you drink must glorify God. You must be wondering, "How?" Firstly, your body is the temple of the Holy Spirit, which means the spirit of God dwells in you, so whatever you do to your body matters to him. It's no longer just your body, it's God's body too; so, be mindful of the food and drinks you consume. Don't eat too much sugary and fatty food that can damage your health later – that does not glorify God. You need your body, and God needs your body too for the great things he wants you to do in his kingdom. A man who is alive and in good health has a greater chance of fulfilling his purpose on earth, but a sick man can barely do anything. God wants you healthy; that is why Jesus took away all of our sicknesses when he got beaten and nailed to the cross.

Daily Do: In all that you do, make sure it represents who you are in Christ. Ask the Holy Spirit to help you out with this.

DAY 38

"FINALLY, BROTHERS, WHATEVER IS TRUE, WHATEVER IS HONORABLE, WHATEVER IS JUST, WHATEVER IS PURE, WHATEVER IS LOVELY, WHATEVER IS COMMENDABLE, IF THERE IS ANY EXCELLENCE, IF THERE IS ANYTHING WORTHY OF PRAISE, THINK ABOUT THESE THINGS." – PHILIPPIANS 4:8

Daily Devotion: Your thoughts are powerful, so much that they can either attract the presence of God or that of the devil. Your thought is like a spiritual magnet; if it is filled with godly and positive substance, it magnetizes the right things for you. Sad thoughts lead to an unhappy and depressing life, but good thoughts to a joyful and peaceful life. That is why the Bible teaches that we must be intentional concerning our thoughts and imaginations. You must intentionally push away wrong thoughts with the words of God, that is, declare the opposite of that thought according to the word of God. For instance "God has not given me the spirit of fear, but the spirit of power, love, and sound mind". When you say that out loud, you deal with thoughts of fear, intimidation, and sadness. You can also declare "The joy of the Lord is my strength" and "I have the mind of Christ; I cast down wrong imaginations".

Make sure you only permit thoughts that are godly, good, lovely, pure, and filled with the truth of God's word.

Daily Do: Confess the words of God every time the wrong thoughts come to you and think about what God says about you daily.

DAY 39

"IF WE CONFESS OUR SINS, HE WILL FORGIVE OUR SINS." – 1 JOHN 1:9

Daily Devotional: God does not condemn or push away anyone that is sincerely sorry for their wrongs and confesses them immediately. Do not feel like God is angry with you and doesn't want you near him when you do something wrong. Quite the opposite, he wants you to run to him whenever you feel helpless in the face of temptations.

If you will confess your sins by saying something like "Lord I'm sorry I lied, please forgive me" Just be sincere with him and he will forgive you instantly – he erases the record of that sin forever.

King David in the Bible was a man who knew how forgiving God is; he always ran to God when he made terrible mistakes, and God continuously forgave him. But make sure you are not repeating the same mistake over and over; be sincere about changing for good. That is why you have the Holy Spirit to ask for help to overcome mistakes and become mature in Christ.

Daily Do: Perhaps, you've done something wrong that made God unhappy with you; confess it now and ask for forgiveness. Take note to do this anytime you go wrong.

DAY 40

"WHATEVER YOU DO, WORK HEARTILY, AS FOR THE LORD AND NOT FOR MEN." – COLOSSIANS 3:23

Daily Devotion: Your whole life belongs to God, which means all your activity must be dedicated to him; he must be pleased with everything you do; whether you are at home, school, church, or anywhere else. See yourself as a worker whose boss is the Lord.

There are a lot of people who hate their bosses and do their work complaining and grumbling. This is not right because we must do all our activities with a cheerful and joyful heart, like it is for God, not actually for men because God is our true reward. So, when your teacher or coach tells you to work hard on something that will make you a better student, do not get angry and hate them for trying to shape you correctly. God is the one training and teaching you through them. Yes! He wants to shape your mind and body according to his plan for your life. As a child of God, your spirit has been renewed when you got born again, but your mind and body take time to get renewed. Do you wonder why your mind needs to be renewed? Well, you must have a healthy mind to fulfill your destiny.

Daily Do: Do all your work daily, knowing that you are doing it for the Lord.

DAY 41

"A NEW COMMAND I GIVE YOU: LOVE ONE ANOTHER. AS I HAVE LOVED YOU, SO YOU MUST LOVE ONE ANOTHER." – JOHN 13:34

Daily Devotional: Love is the most common language in the world. Everyone wants to be loved, even if some do not admit it. God created man out of love. God also created man for love. He loves everyone just as they are, and by his love, he seeks to save everyone from the bondage of sin. So, we are expected to love people too just as we are loved.

A young boy named Chris always heard his pastor at church talk about the importance of showing love to people. So, he decided that he would show love at every chance that he gets. One day, while riding his bike on the street, he saw an old woman whose walking stick go stuck in a cracked spot on the sidewalk. For a moment, Chris looked away and kept riding, but the Holy Spirit brought back the words of his pastor to his mind "Show love to others as God shows love to you". Chris stopped and turned around to help the woman. She was so happy that she blessed him with all her heart. Chris felt a huge wave of joy and fulfillment on his way back home. It sure pays to love others with the love of God.

Daily Do: Love is a gift you have in your heart. Pour it out to others every day, and you'll make the world so much better.

DAY 42

"CALL TO ME IN TIMES OF TROUBLE. I WILL SAVE YOU, AND YOU WILL HONOR ME." – PSALM 50:15

Daily Devotion: Caleb could see the worried looks on his parents' faces when he got back from school. When he asked them what the problem was, they told him it was nothing for him to bother about. So he forgot about it and went to bed. The next day, he heard the doorbell ring and decided to go check who might be visiting their home so early. He heard some voices as he walked down to the living room; he saw a strange man discussing with his parents. Caleb hid behind a door to listen. A few minutes later, the man left. Now, Caleb understood why his parents were worried – They were about to lose their home.

Caleb took out his Bible and opened that scripture, he read out loud "Call to me in times of trouble. I will save you, and you will honor me" Caleb prayed to God that night to save his family from the trouble they were facing. He prayed for God to help them recover their house. After praying, he gave thanks to God for listening to him and went cheerfully to sleep. The next couple of days, a letter came to their house stating that their debt had been cleared. God used the most unexpected means to help them out. Caleb's parents didn't understand why the bank canceled their debt. But Caleb knew it was the Lord. He revealed this to his parents, and together, they never stopped giving thanks, worshipping, and reading the Bible daily. What did you learn from Caleb's story?

Daily Do: Call on the Lord when you or your loved ones are in trouble, and he will come with great deliverance. It might not happen the same way it happened in the story, but God will always answer you.

DAY 43

"DON'T BE AFRAID BECAUSE I AM WITH YOU."
– ISAIAH 43:5

Daily Devotion: Have you ever been terrified of something or someone? What made you so afraid?

Let me tell you what fear is: it is a lie of the devil. You and God are inseparable, and he will never allow anything to hurt you. He says "Don't be afraid because I am with you" This alone should assure you that fear does not belong to your heart, only love. The best way to let go of fear is to let the love of God fill your heart daily. The Bible says "perfect love casts out all fears".

Stay confident that the King of Kings is always with you, and no monster, demon, or any other evil can come near you. Stop watching scary movies, it will only attract fear into your heart. For God has not given you the spirit of fear, but of power, love, and sound mind. If God doesn't give fear, then who does? You guessed that right! It's the enemy. So, don't take anything from him; stay under the protection of God's power and love.

Daily Do: Whenever you get scared of anything, remember that the Lord has said "Don't be afraid because I am with you".

DAY 44

"SO ENCOURAGE EACH OTHER AND BUILD EACH OTHER UP." – 1 THESSALONIANS 5:11

Daily Devotion: We all need someone to talk to. Imagine a young boy like you who never spoke to anyone, nor had any friends. He wouldn't learn anything new, have great experiences, or become the best version of himself. You become a better person when you create good relationships with others and show love, care, and kindness. Likewise, the Bible teaches us to encourage and build each other up as a family in Christ. God doesn't want anyone to stay alone in their room and be depressed; he wants us to remind each other of his WORD, which can build us up in times of challenges.

If you ever see someone feeling down, encourage them with the word of God, bring a smile to their face, and give them hope.

Daily Do: Encourage yourself and others with the word of God. Do not get sad and worried about anything.

DAY 45

"LOVE YOUR NEIGHBOR AS YOURSELF."
— MATTHEW 22:39

Daily Devotion: You love yourself right? You would do anything to please yourself – eat that food you crave, get that toy you love, and wear your favorite clothes and shoes.

It's absolutely normal to love yourself. But you can go wrong by loving just yourself and not others. Matthew 22:39 as shown above are the direct words of Jesus; he knows that you love yourself, but he commands you also to love your neighbor just as you love yourself. Your neighbors are not only those living around your house, but every person out there in the world is your neighbor. You must love them as you love yourself; you must be able to give another kid one of your favorite toys or share your lovely meal. GOD IS LOVE, and he lives in you. So, share Love today.

Daily Do: Do an act of love daily; if there is something you would do for yourself, do it for others.

DAY 46

"SO GOD CREATED MANKIND IN HIS OWN IMAGE, IN THE IMAGE AND LIKENESS OF GOD HE CREATED HIM; MALE AND FEMALE HE CREATED THEM." – GENESIS 1:27

Daily Devotion: God created man and woman in his image and likeness. A man is a MAN, and a woman is a WOMAN; there is no mix-up because that was God's idea. The differences between a man and a woman were intentionally done by God. He created them to represent the various sides of his personality. That is why the way a man thinks and reacts is different from the way a woman thinks and reacts to situations. Appreciate the fact that you were created as a man, and also respect and appreciate every woman you know and will ever meet. We are God's unique idea; we are an expression of his image and creativity. We are his beautiful work of art that he loves so dearly. A woman is unique in her way, and a man is also unique in his way. Any idea about man and woman that isn't the same as God's idea is a big lie. Stick with the truth of God's word, and you will be safe from the wrong ideas in the world today.

Daily Do: Thank God for his great idea of creating humanity, and making you a part of his great plan to restore it into its original form as in the 'beginning'.

DAY 47

"JESUS ANSWERED, 'I AM THE WAY AND THE TRUTH AND THE LIFE. NO ONE COMES TO THE FATHER EXCEPT THROUGH ME.'" – JOHN 14:6

Daily Devotion: There is no other name a man can call upon for salvation except JESUS. He is the way, the truth, and the life. No man can have a relationship with God without first going through Jesus. The devil has deceived the world that people can serve God through one prophet or holy man that isn't Jesus. He has deceived people to believe that Jesus is an option among many others.

I want you to know that Jesus is the son of God who was sent to die for the sins of humanity. Jesus is the expression of God's love, grace, and mercy to man. Take note of these in your diary:

- Jesus is the only way to the only living God who created all things.
- Truth can only be found when following Jesus because he is TRUTH.
- Eternal life is found in Jesus.

There is no other way of knowing God the father except you go through God the Son, who is Jesus. There is so much about God that you will get to know as you grow in your relationship with him. The more you stay with God and study your Bible, the more you will grow in your knowledge and understanding of who he is.

Daily Do: Pray for those who do not know Jesus yet as their Lord and Savior. Ask that the light of God will shine upon their hearts.

DAY 48

"I KNOW THE PLANS I HAVE IN MIND FOR YOU, DECLARES THE LORD; THEY ARE PLANS FOR PEACE, NOT DISASTER, TO GIVE YOU A FUTURE FILLED WITH HOPE." – JEREMIAH 29:11

Daily Devotion: Before God created you, he had you in his mind; he knew you, and he had a perfect plan written down for you. His plans are good, and not evil because he has a future filled with hope for you. He wants the best for you, but the question is: Do you want God's plan?

If you do, then you wouldn't struggle with him on the process and training he is taking you through in life. He wants to teach you how to be responsible, respectful, loving, kind, selfless, and faithful. So, he does this through the adults in your life, especially your parents, teachers, pastors, and coaches.

As you grow older, remember that God has a plan for you, and you can only fulfill your destiny if you stick to his plan.

Daily Do: Say this prayer "Lord I thank you for the plans you have in mind for me. I submit to them today and for the rest of my life. So help me Lord in Jesus' name" Amen.

DAY 49

"A FOOL DOESN'T LIKE A FATHER'S INSTRUCTION, BUT THOSE WHO HEED CORRECTION ARE MATURE."
– PROVERBS 15:5

Daily Devotion: It's considered foolishness when a young child doesn't take heed to corrections. Many times, corrections are made to save you from terrible mistakes in the future. When you are being corrected by an adult in your life or anyone at all, make sure you listen attentively and do the right thing. Do not repeat the same mistake you got corrected over. It's a sign of immaturity and foolishness. As a child of God, you must be humble enough to admit your wrongs and do things right as you are instructed, whether at home, school, church, or anywhere else.

God is a Father, and he will always seek to correct you when you go on the wrong path, many times through the Bible, parents, and leaders.
You only know better when you are open to learning. The Bible calls a man who listens to correction "Wise". Decide to be a wise child who will eventually grow into a wise gentleman.

A wise man never makes bad choices because he always seeks the face of God before doing anything in life.

Daily Do: Ask the Lord to help you to always listen to corrections when you get them.

DAY 50

"I'VE COMMANDED YOU TO BE BRAVE AND STRONG, HAVEN'T I? DON'T BE ALARMED OR TERRIFIED, BECAUSE THE LORD YOUR GOD IS WITH YOU WHEREVER YOU GO." – JOSHUA 1:9

Daily Devotion: God has commanded us to stay brave and strong wherever we go because he is with us. A lot of people are terrified of heights, closed spaces, pools, animals, clowns, the police, robbers, darkness, viruses, and so many other things. When God is with you, nothing shall by any means hurt you.

Do not entertain or welcome fear into your life, no matter what happens on the earth. Live with the confidence that God goes with you wherever you are; on the plane, boat, car, train, or bike.
In the Bible, Prophet Elisha was once surrounded by his enemies, and his servant was scared that they might get killed. But the Prophet told him that the angels that are with the two of them are much more than those enemies.

Angels have been commanded by God to keep watch over you, while God himself is still with you. He does not keep his eyes off you, and neither do his angels. They will come to defend you against your enemies when necessary. Many times, you are not even aware when this happens. Just stay brave, strong, and peaceful always. He's got you!

Daily Do: Thank God for always protecting and defending you wherever you go in life.

DAY 51

"GIVE THANKS TO THE LORD BECAUSE HE IS GOOD. GOD'S FAITHFUL LOVE LASTS FOREVER!" – PSALM 136:1

Daily Devotion: Thanksgiving is so important to God. It proves that you recognize what he has done for you, and you are grateful. God deserves to be thanked through our prayers, praises, and worship because he is good and his faithfulness lasts forever. He never leaves nor abandons his child. He has never failed anyone, and he won't start with you; he will do all that he promised in the scriptures. People can fail and disappoint you, but God is the friend that sticks closer than anyone else ever could.

Daily Do: List out at least three things you know God has done for you and your family. Give thanks to God for each of them.

DAY 52

"ALL WHO ARE LED BY GOD'S SPIRIT ARE GOD'S SONS AND DAUGHTERS." – ROMANS 8:14

Daily Devotion: Victor could sense strongly in his heart that the Holy Spirit wanted him to preach the gospel to one of his classmates at his high school but every time he got to school, he never did. One day his coach called him aside after football practice and told him that he had a significant dream about him. In the dream, Victor seemed to have disobeyed his Dad.

After the coach was done, Victor knew the meaning of the dream. If God was truly his father as he always called him, then a true son should listen and obey the voice of his father. Victor went ahead to preach to the student, and it turned out that the student needed Victor to speak to him. The student was depressed, and he had no real family or friends; since Victor obeyed God's voice not only did he help out his fellow student who was struggling but made a friend along the way.

Listening and obeying the voice of the Spirit of God is only done by true sons of God. What parent would be please to have a child that ignores and disobeys their instructions? Scripture says "For as many that are led by the spirit of God, they are the sons of God".

Daily Do: Say this prayer "Dear Holy Spirit, help me to hear you every time you speak to me. Help me also to obey your every word, that I may not grieve you."

DAY 53

"CLOTHE YOURSELVES WITH HUMILITY TOWARD EACH OTHER. GOD STANDS AGAINST THE PROUD, BUT HE GIVES FAVOR TO THE HUMBLE." – 1 PETER 5:5

Daily Devotional: Humility is one of the greatest virtue you could have as a child of God. Have you seen a young man boasting about the riches he inherited from his father?

There once was a boy named Sam, who came from a rich home, and he always got what he wanted no matter what. He was the biggest bully in school, and he made a lot of boys serve him for money, including doing his homework. Remember, he's just living off his father's riches, he barely knows anything about getting a job. But one day, his father lost a huge part of his money and had to sell his house and cars to pay off his debts. The luxurious life Sam loved came crashing down before his eyes; soon he couldn't boss people around anymore. It's just as the Bible says "Pride goes before a fall". A proud person is like a man standing on a skyscraper built on sand; when heavy rain falls, the building will come crashing down. Do not put your trust in the physical things you have – your good grades, clothes, toys, shoes, money, jewelry, etc. Your trust should always be in God and his faithfulness. It's like standing on a solid rock that never crashes down. God doesn't like arrogant people, but he honors humble people. Jesus was a humble man on earth; he was a king that came to serve.

Daily Do: A humble man always respects authority. He never boasts about what he has. Live your life daily in humility, and the Lord will honor you.

DAY 54

"BELIEVE IN THE LORD JESUS CHRIST, AND YOU WILL BE SAVED." – ACTS 16:31

Daily Devotional: When Jesus was nailed to the cross, two criminals were also nailed to other crosses by his left and right sides. One of them mocked Jesus by telling him to come down from the cross, and help him and his fellow criminal down too. He continued that if Jesus was truly the son of God, he would do it. Jesus never tried to prove anything to anyone who disbelieved him. Surprisingly the second man believed that Jesus is who he says he is: THE SON OF GOD. So, he told Jesus to remember him in heaven that day. And Jesus promised him that a spot has already been reserved for him at the moment he believed.

This is beautiful because it proves that even the worst criminal can get saved if they believe in Jesus as the son of God.

You believed, and therefore you got saved. Your home is in heaven, not hell. You have been given the power over every work of the devil since the moment you got saved. Preach the gospel of Christ to unsaved people, and let them have a home in heaven because of your obedience.

Daily Do: Tell someone about Jesus today.

DAY 55

"THE LORD BLESS YOU AND KEEP YOU."
– NUMBERS 6:24

Daily Devotional: God constantly desires to bless his children; His blessings bring goodness, prosperity, success, joy, and peace. Who doesn't want that?

The more we draw closer to God and ask for his blessings, the more his blessings get poured out on us. Like a cool rain-fall, God showers his blessings to bring comfort and freedom in times of trouble. This is a spiritual form of comfort and freedom – it occurs when you are free from the chains and lies of the enemy over your life. When you feel bad, or in need of something, you can ask him to pour out his blessings on you, and you will have it. You will feel his peace because his arms will be wrapped around you to comfort you.

Also, God doesn't just bless you, he keeps you. Some people are kept by unforgiveness and bitterness, while some are kept by their fleshy desires, depression, and darkness – they live inside of these things. But the one, who is kept by the Lord, lives and grows in him.

Note that your future is blessed and kept by the Lord, for you belong to him.

Daily Do: Say to yourself "I am blessed and kept by the Lord all the days of my life, in Jesus' name" Amen.

DAY 56

"HOW CAN A YOUNG MAN KEEP HIS WAY PURE? BY GUARDING IT ACCORDING TO YOUR WORD." – PSALM 119:9

Daily Devotion: Every young man faces difficulties in living a pure life. He will always come across many temptations to sin against God. But when he studies and obeys the word of God, which is the Bible, he will be able to escape safely.

As you grow older, there will be many things that will try to draw your heart away from God, but when you know God's word, you will not be deceived and displease God. His word is like a warrior's shield that protects your heart from sin.

The world believes that as a kid, you are free to live a sinful life, free to enjoy what the enemy brings to you, and when you become much older; you can then decide to follow God. This is far from the truth – God wants you to live for him now that you are very young – the earlier you become a child of God, the better your adulthood would be.

Daily Do: Study the book of Psalm chapter one, memorize it and make sure you are that righteous boy that does not hang with sinful people. Also, tell God to help you keep your heart pure daily.

DAY 57

"BE KIND AND COMPASSIONATE TO ONE ANOTHER, FORGIVING EACH OTHER, JUST AS IN CHRIST GOD FORGAVE YOU." – EPHESIANS 4:32

Daily Devotion: God forgave you of your sins through the sacrifice of our Lord Jesus on the cross. He wants you to do the same with others – your family, friends, schoolmates, teachers, coaches, and strangers. Do you remember a line in the Lord's Prayer that says "... forgive us of our trespasses as we forgive those who trespass against us"? Trespass here means sins, wrongs, or hurts. If you don't let go of the pain someone caused you, and you choose to pay back by hurting them, God will not be able to forgive you. We are called to love others because Christ showed his love to us.

The word 'compassionate' is the feeling you get when you see someone suffering or in pain, and you want to help out or rescue them. Jesus showed kindness and compassion when he was on earth. You can do the same too.

Daily Do: Choose to forgive anyone that hurts you from today. Do something nice for them, and pray for them.

DAY 58

"ALL PEOPLE HAVE SINNED AND COME SHORT OF THE GLORY OF GOD." – ROMANS 3:23

Daily Devotional: Do you know that it's not just terrible sinners such as murderers, idolaters, liars, etc. that need salvation? Even people who seem to be so nice and never commit any evil also need saving. Why do you think we all need to be saved? Well, when Adam and Eve sinned by disobeying God, they not just attracted curses upon themselves but upon every human. So, every human that is born on the earth from that day is born a sinner. Sin flowed from the very first humans down to every child that would ever be born. The only different person was Jesus. And that is because he is God who came in a human body. Every person has sinned and come short of God's glory, so we all need to be saved from sin whether we are brought up with good manners or terrible ones, whether nice or mean, as long as a human soul has not been surrendered to Jesus, he is a sinner and needs salvation. God embraces every human because he loves us, and all he wants is that we come to him the way we are and get our sins washed away by the blood of Jesus. So, it's not about doing good things first, but being saved first. When one is saved, the spirit of God that comes to dwell inside of him will move him to do good things easily, except he doesn't want to. But no one has the spirit of God and comfortably does evil. It's not the nature of God to do evil, so it's not in the nature of a child of God either. That is why you do only what the spirit of God in you leads you to do. And how do you know what he doesn't want? You know when you feel uneasy and uncomfortable after doing a certain act. You are one with him.

Daily Do: Do you know anyone that has probably never given their life to Jesus? Pray that they experience God's salvation and become one with God.

DAY 59

"I AM WITH YOU ALWAYS." – MATTHEW 28:20

Daily Devotional: After Jesus rose from the dead and was about to ascend to heaven, he baptized his disciples in the name of the Father, and the Son, and the Holy Spirit, then he commanded them to preach the gospel he taught them to the entire world. He gave them the power to heal the sick, cast out devils, pray in new tongues, and trample on snakes and scorpions; that is, they have the power over evil and more (Check out Mark 16:15-18).

Although Jesus sent his disciples on a life-long mission, he added "I am with you always, even to the end of the age". He never sent them out to preach to the world alone, he promised to be with them throughout their journeys, and he kept his words.

Likewise, Jesus is calling you to live your life for his glory, and preach to others about him; and he will always be there to guide, protect, and provide for you until you are done with your mission on earth and go to meet him in heaven.

Daily Do: Pray this prayer to Jesus "Thank you Lord for calling me according to your purpose. Help me to fulfill my destiny and make you proud." Amen.

DAY 60

"THIS IS THE DAY THE LORD HAS MADE; LET US REJOICE AND BE GLAD IN IT." – PSALM 118:24

Daily Devotional: You slept last night and awoke this morning, right? Of course, you did, which is why you can read this devotional. God was the one who made you sleep because you needed to rest, and he woke you up to see a brand new day. Never be ungrateful for the gift of life that God has given to you; never think it is normal because not everyone has that privilege/opportunity (Read Psalms 3:5, Psalms 4:8, and Psalms 127:2).

Each day is a day that the Lord has made, and you should rejoice and be glad in it. Give thanks to God every morning when you rise and receive his strength to carry out all your activities for each day. You have the gift of life to live for God and bring glory to his name by showing his love to others and growing in your relationship with him. No day must go to waste.

Daily Do: See each day as an opportunity for God to express himself to the world through you. Be grateful for each day. Now, go and win with Jesus!

DAY 61

"TRUST IN THE LORD WITH ALL YOUR HEART AND LEAN NOT ON YOUR UNDERSTANDING; IN ALL YOUR WAYS SUBMIT TO HIM, AND HE WILL MAKE YOUR PATHS STRAIGHT." – PROVERBS 3:5-6

Daily Devotional: You must learn to trust God in all that you do – including everything you think you can figure out on your own. Learn to do this with all your heart, not keeping anything away from him. Speak to God about the things you plan to do; never do them on your own. He is always looking forward to your invitation, so do not count him out or ignore him. When you tell him everything you go through, he will direct you to the right path. You know, God never makes mistakes, so you are sure to be on a path of peace and joy. He will never guide you to do something that will hurt or endanger you. He is your best friend, so treat him as such.

Daily Do: Pray to God about something you want to do. Choose to believe and trust him to guide you.

DAY 62

"IN THE BEGINNING, GOD CREATED THE HEAVENS AND THE EARTH." – GENESIS 1:1

Daily Devotional: Many kids are filled with questions about the existence of God. Some ask "Where did God come from". Others ask "how does God look?"

You do not have to bother your innocent mind with questions like that. Just read your Bible and listen to those who teach you the word of God; and you will begin to understand who God is, little by little. You can only know him through his word.

God is God, he is the creator of all things. There is nothing that exists without God; humans, the earth, and all that is in it, the universe, and heaven (where God dwells). That is why he calls himself "I AM THAT I AM". He is the beginning and the end of all things; He existed before anything began, and he will continue to exist even when all things no longer exist (when the world ends).

You come from this mighty God, and He calls you his own. Whoa! Isn't that the greatest blessing ever?

There is no other God except the living God, and this is a big truth that the world has still not understood. But congrats! You know this truth.

Daily Do: Study the account of the creation in the book of Genesis.

DAY 63

"THE LORD KNOWS THE WAY OF THE RIGHTEOUS, BUT THE WAY OF THE WICKED WILL PERISH."
– PSALM 1:6

Daily Devotional: God sees and approves of the ways of a righteous man and woman. But the way of the wicked will perish, which means it will be destroyed.

Now, what are the ways of a righteous person? The ways of the righteous are the way of the Lord; a holy way, a good and perfect way.

The ways of the wicked include their evil acts. For example, a wicked man will steal something that belongs to another man just to get what he wants. A wicked woman is capable of destroying the reputation of another woman by gossiping. Wickedness is the overall act of thinking and acting in a way that is against God's will. It is a means of gaining satisfaction from causing others to suffer or even merely supporting it. One who supports the wicked acts of a person is just like them because it's not just the act but the heart.

Daily Do: Pray this prayer: "Thank you Lord for making me righteous. Help me to make my ways and always acts right in your sight" Amen.

DAY 64

"TRUST IN THE LORD FOREVER, FOR THE LORD GOD IS AN EVERLASTING ROCK." – ISAIAH 26:4

Daily Devotional: To trust in the Lord means to keep your heart and mind on him, shoving aside the storms of life that seek to make you fearful and doubtful.

Have you ever seen a huge rock that is bigger than the size of a mansion? Those kinds of rocks are hard to destroy. The rain, thunder, lightning, and floods cannot shake its foundation, move it or wash it away. Same way, God is like a rock, but he's even greater because he is an everlasting rock; He is faithful, and you can always count on him. When your life is hidden in Christ, you will always be shielded from the attacks and troubles of the enemy – Satan can try his best, but he can't get you. This is a promise that lasts forever.

Daily Do: Trust in the Lord to come through for you in every area of your life.

DAY 65

"THE LORD, YOUR GOD, WILL GO AHEAD OF YOU. HE WILL FIGHT FOR YOU." – DEUTERONOMY 1:30

Daily Devotional: Have you read the story of the Israelites? The way God used Moses to set them free from slavery in Egypt was incredible! So, in the Bible verse, we are looking at today, Moses was reminding the Israelites that the Lord will go ahead of them and fight for them as he did in Egypt.

You see, the Israelites were fond of forgetting the incredible miracles that God did for them whenever they faced a challenge. They continued to sin against God despite his goodness towards them. This hurts God every time.

I want you to learn a lesson from this; never forget what God did in your past, and stay confident that he will always go ahead of you to fight your battles. And you know well that God always wins!

Daily Do: Pray to God now about any challenges you or your loved ones are facing. Tell him you trust him to fight every battle as he did for his people in the Bible.

DAY 66

"PEOPLE LOOK AT THE OUTSIDE OF A PERSON, BUT THE LORD LOOKS AT THE HEART." – 1 SAMUEL 16:7

Daily Devotional: This is so true! Can you read the mind of the person next to you? Sit still and focus on him/her. Did you get anything? I'm sure not! You have no idea if they are planning on doing something good or bad in the next minute. It's the same when you are on the train, on a bus, in a park, at school, at church, and wherever you find yourself. You don't know what's going on in people's minds, but God does. That sounds impossible, but with God all things are possible. Only he can read every single human, like a book. Yet, he does not hate anyone; instead, he loves and shows mercy.

People judge each other based on what they see, but God judges based on the heart. A person may not look so nice on the outside, and people may assume they are unfriendly or probably a criminal, but God sees what no one sees – the heart of that human.

Daily Do: Ask God to reveal the true nature of people you meet, in order not to judge too quickly and wrongly.

DAY 67

"TELL YOUR SINS TO EACH OTHER. AND PRAY FOR EACH OTHER SO YOU MAY BE HEALED. THE PRAYER FROM THE HEART OF A MAN RIGHT WITH GOD HAS MUCH POWER." – JAMES 5:16

Daily Devotional: The church of Christ is also called the body of Christ. This includes every church he established, not the ones created by men's will. You see, when God builds something, he makes sure he defends and preserves it, but when man builds something that God didn't permit him to build, he will face the troubles that come on his own. The Bible says "obedience is better than sacrifice."

So, as the body of Christ, we are expected to pray for each other and encourage one another. If anyone feels guilty about something he did wrong, he can tell his sins to the leader in his church and he will be advised to seek God's forgiveness, and will also be shown how to resist such sin and live a godly life. This was what they did in the churches during the days of the Apostles; the church was a family, and it still is.

I also want you to know that prayer is one of the greatest weapons you have as a Christian. Never stop praying no matter the circumstances because the prayer of a righteous man has the power to make amazing things happen for God's kingdom.

Daily Do: Make a decision today to share your challenges with your Pastor or Bible school teacher, and make sure to pray every day, anywhere, and anytime.

DAY 68

"GOD IS OUR REFUGE AND STRENGTH, ALWAYS READY TO HELP IN TIMES OF TROUBLE." – PSALM 46:1

Daily Devotional: God is your refuge and strength, and he is always ready to help you in times of trouble. A refuge is a safe place you can hide, a haven, a shelter. More like a safe cave in a rock where soldiers hid from their enemies in the Bible.

A great example in our current time is a refugee camp. This is a safe place where refugees hide from troubles or war going on in their country. Refugees are people seeking shelter from a foreign country. So, countries that are willing to help these people, build refugee camps. In these camps, the refugees get a place to sleep, food to eat, water to drink, and every other basic thing they may need to survive.

God is even much better than a refugee camp; he's willing to protect just anyone that comes to him, not considering their race, culture, religion, and sins. As long as they come to him, his arms are wide open to receive them. He is a reliable refuge who strengthens anyone that comes to him. He washes away sins and clothes them with a garment of holiness.

Daily Do: Pray this prayer "Thank you Lord for being my refuge. I know I am safe in your hands. Give me the grace to stay with you for the rest of my life".

DAY 69

"CHILDREN, OBEY YOUR PARENTS IN EVERYTHING, FOR THIS PLEASES THE LORD." – COLOSSIANS 3:20

Daily Devotion: The Bible commands children to obey their parents in all things. As long as you depend on your parents for all your needs, including the roof over your head, the food you eat, clothes you wear, your school and medical expenses, and many other things you don't even know – they have the right to tell you what to and what not to do. Do your chores, and be thankful for all that your parents do for you. This is the will of God for you, and he will be pleased when you obey.

Daily Do: Your parents have sacrificed so much for you. Do something kind for them today, and do things the way they like them to be done. Put a smile on mom and dad's faces.

DAY 70

"YOU WILL CALL MY NAME. YOU WILL COME TO ME AND PRAY TO ME. AND I WILL LISTEN TO YOU." – JEREMIAH 29:12

Daily Devotion: When God made this promised to prophet Jeremiah, he had you in mind. So, this is also his promise to you; He wants you to know that you have a purpose in him before you were born, and because his heart is joined with yours in his purpose, you will always seek for him, and there will be a hunger inside your soul that will move you to seek God, and when you do, he will listen attentively.

You and God are partners here on earth; he leads the team while you follow him. Sticking with your leader (God) will keep you on the safer side of life. And you are sure to fulfill your purpose when you do this.

Daily Do: Come boldly to God daily and let him know the desires of your heart. Pray with an assurance that he hears you.

DAY 71

"OUR HIGH PRIEST IS ABLE TO UNDERSTAND OUR WEAKNESSES." – HEBREWS 4:15

Daily Devotional: Jesus Christ is our faithful high priest; he is seated at the right hand of God, praying for us daily. He once lived on earth, so he is familiar with every human experience. This means he perfectly understands what we go through as humans. Jesus knows how you feel when you get emotionally hurt, betrayed, and even little things such as having a headache, a wound, or a scratch on your knees and elbows. He had his favorite meals, brushed his teeth, and took his bath daily, he lived a normal human life as you do. Remember, he was born just like you, so he had a childhood like you are having right now. He had friends whom he laughed, cried, and played with. They loved him because he was just so different; he was good and kind, he was the exact image of God, and still is (Hebrews 1:3).

Jesus knows how it feels to fight sins and temptations, yet he never gave in at any point. He resisted every sin and remained holy all his life. He is our great example, and we must follow his pattern. We should strive to model our lives after his.

Daily Do: Say this to Jesus "Lord, I believe you are my high priest, and you can relate with all my experiences and weaknesses. Thank you because I am becoming more like you daily with the help of your Holy Spirit" Amen.

DAY 72

"AND WE KNOW THAT FOR THOSE WHO LOVE GOD, ALL THINGS WORK TOGETHER FOR GOOD."
– ROMANS 8:28

Daily Devotional: Nothing just happens! Every event in life has a reason, a purpose for occurring at the time it occurred. For instance, the pandemic happened at a specific time, and it was meant to happen; because it's one of the major signs of the end time (Matthew 24). Everything that happens physically has firstly happened spiritually. I know this might be a lot to take in but be assured that God doesn't do evil; the devil does. God loves humans, the devil doesn't. This is why God shows mercy by not judging the earth despite all the wickedness in it, whereas the devil keeps pouring out all sorts of hate and bad events. But, no matter what the enemy does on the earth, those of us who love God will never be victims because all things work together for our good. Although problems surround us, we will never be afraid or have anxiety; God will always work things out in our favor. What may seem like a big problem now will turn out to become a blessing soon.

Daily Do: Say this out loud "All things are working together for my good because I am a child of God" Remember these words every time there's a challenge around you.

DAY 73

"BUT HE GAVE UP HIS PLACE WITH GOD AND MADE HIMSELF NOTHING. HE WAS BORN AS A MAN AND BECAME LIKE A SERVANT." – PHILIPPIANS 2:7

Daily Devotional: This scripture above talks about the humility and meekness of Jesus; a mighty person who gave up all his Glory and majesty to become a human; an unlimited God who limited himself by living a human life. That must have been so hard for him. Yet, he didn't think twice before making such a big sacrifice of love.

Imagine a mighty king of a famous kingdom who decided to stripe off his royal garments and crown. Then he chose to wear cheap clothing and live in a small hut with normal people, just because he loved them and desired to bring them along to his palace. Could you do such if you were the king? Maybe not. No one is willing to leave luxury for poverty, or power and strength for weakness. Everyone wants the good things, a comfortable life. But Jesus gave up his comfort zone (heaven) to come here on earth for your salvation. All Glory and Honor be to his name!

Daily Do: Study the first chapter of the book of Hebrews and meditate on the person of Jesus.

DAY 74

"JESUS STRETCHED OUT HIS HAND AND TOUCHED HIM, SAYING, "I AM WILLING; BE CLEANSED." AND IMMEDIATELY, HIS LEPROSY WAS CLEANSED."
– MATTHEW 8:3

Daily Devotional: Sometimes, we have requests we want to give to God, but then we ask "Will God do this for me?" We fight so many thoughts that make us doubt if God is willing to answer some kind of prayer. But the truth is, if it's something truly important to you, he will never turn a deaf ear to your request. God is always willing to heal and deliver you whenever you ask him. This is no excuse for you to ask God for unreasonable things; he can't give you what is against his plan for you, or something you are not ready for. An example of this is you praying to own a car at your current age. That's not a prayer to be considered because there is a perfect time for everything.

Jesus granted the request of the leprous man in the book of Mathew 8:3, and the man was completely healed and made whole. His life changed forever; he was no longer going to be an outcast that people ran away from. He received freedom through healing. During those days in the Bible, people with leprosy (a skin disease that had no cure) were usually sent out of their homes and villages in order not to infect others. But while people avoided them, Jesus came close to them, touched them, and healed them when they asked for his help. Jesus showed compassion for the sick; He has given you the power to do the same, and heal them as he did by the Holy Spirit.

Daily Do: Is there anyone sick around you? Pray for them that they get healed in Jesus' name.

DAY 75

"AND HE SAID, "COME!" AND PETER GOT OUT OF THE BOAT, AND WALKED ON THE WATER AND CAME TOWARD JESUS." – MATTHEW 14:29

Daily Devotional: This passage of the Bible represents the step of faith you should take as a believer in the middle of storms. Look at Peter; he stepped out of the boat when Jesus said "Come", and a miracle happened at that moment; Peter began to do what he had never done before – He walked on water.

Today, Jesus is telling you to come – Come out of your fears, shame, pain, failures, and problems. You may not understand what it's like to have all these issues right now, but a few years from now, you will. And you need God to carry you through those times. So, what you are learning right now is called advanced teaching. I'm preparing you for the future you are about to step into. A man who is prepared before going into a battle always has a greater chance of winning.

Daily Do: I challenge you today to step out and walk on waters as you journey through life.

DAY 76

"AND HE HEALED MANY WHO WERE ILL WITH VARIOUS DISEASES, AND CAST OUT MANY DEMONS, AND HE WAS NOT PERMITTING THE DEMONS TO SPEAK, BECAUSE THEY KNEW WHO HE WAS." – MARK 1:34

Daily Devotional: Jesus healed so many people almost every day. Whenever he traveled to a town – which he did a lot – several sick, lame, and demon-possessed people were brought to him to get healed and free. He never turned them down because he had great love and compassion for them. Even when he got tired, he never stopped helping and healing people until his job was completed each day. He always put the needs of others before his – An act of love and selflessness that we should all imitate. That is, we must love and serve people in the best way we can, just as our savior did.

You must be wondering why the scripture you read above said "He was not permitting the demons to speak because they knew who he was". Well, Jesus didn't want his identity revealed to people; he wanted to keep things quiet about himself. After all, he knew that fame can be distracting, and he was careful not to let his fame get the best of him. And although he tried to stay unpopular, the news about him began to spread all over the earth. This is why he always retreated to a quiet place to pray alone after a long and busy day. This is something very important for every Christian – Finding a quiet place to spend time with God every day. Doing this strengthens our relationship with God.

Daily Do: Do you have a special time in the day that you set aside to spend with God? If you don't, set up a time now, and be faithful to it.

DAY 77

"REJOICE IN THE LORD ALWAYS; AGAIN, I WILL SAY REJOICE!" – PHILIPPIANS 4:4

Daily Devotional: The word Rejoice was mentioned 183 times in the Bible. That's a lot! So, It must be really important.

God continues to emphasize that we rejoice in all that we do. Take a look at the word Joy; it is related to rejoicing. This means we rejoice only when there's Joy in our hearts.

So, where does joy come from? Well, Joy comes from God; It is an assurance in our hearts that God is good, and that things can only get better for us. Joy bubbles in the spirit of a man. It's not the same as happiness. You are happy only when you get something you like or want.

Joy requires that you rejoice even in the face of tribulation or problems. The Bible also says "in all things give thanks to God". So, while you rejoice, you must also give thanks. Come to think of it; it does seem impossible to rejoice and complain at the same time, right?

When you rejoice, the presence of God and his angel will be attracted to you, which can lead to powerful miracles happening in your life and family. Being sad and gloomy attracts the wrong spirit, and I'm sure you don't want that.

Daily Do: Make it a habit to rejoice daily. Let God know that you are joyful and thankful to him in all things.

DAY 78

"YOU ARE THE LIGHT OF THE WORLD. A CITY SET ON A HILL CANNOT BE HIDDEN." – MATTHEW 5:14

Daily Devotional: Salt is used to heal wounds, and give good taste to something. The world is wounded and decayed in many ways because of the evils that fill it, and only Christians who take their place as the salt of the earth will bring healing to many lands.

Likewise, we are the light of the world. We bring light upon every darkness that has covered the world because of sin. This is why Jesus called us to preach the gospel in every nation. His light inside of us can only spread if we preach to others and lead them to Jesus.
Imagine if a thousand Christians spread light to a thousand sinners, who get saved and then spread what they heard to another thousand, who also do the same, and so on until the whole earth is filled with the light and the glory of the Lord.

Daily Do: Be a salt that heals people's hearts, and a light that chases every darkness wherever you go.

DAY 79

WHEN I AM AFRAID, I PUT MY TRUST IN YOU."
– PSALM 56:3

Daily Devotional: We all have our different fears in life, but the Bible made us know that when we are afraid, we can count on God to help us out of it. There is nothing you are afraid of that God cannot handle. He constantly says "Fear not because I am with you".

David in Psalm 56, is telling God that whenever he gets afraid – probably when his enemies surround him in a battle – He will put his trust in God. King David wrote this at a time when he fought so many battles. And although he was a great warrior, he admitted that a lot of times he also got afraid as a normal human would.

God always came through for King David because he trusted in his (God's) faithfulness. A man who trusts God gets the best of God, but a man who doubts God's ability will never get anything from God. We can only please God when we trust and have faith that he can do all things.

Daily Do: Tell God now about anything you seem to be afraid of, no matter how big or small, tell him. Surrender that fear/fears to him, and begin to trust him to deliver you from them all.

DAY 80

"DO NOT FORGET TO DO GOOD TO OTHERS. AND SHARE WITH THEM WHAT YOU HAVE."
– HEBREWS 13:16

Daily Devotional: It's vanity (useless) when we give praises, worship, and thanks to God, but we leave our fellow humans in need when we have something to give. The Bible says "God loves a cheerful giver". You are more like Jesus when you give to others because he also gave up his life for the whole world, including you.

God knows that people may offend/annoy you sometimes, but he wants you to be good at all times. It will not be easy, but he's got your back, and he will help you to be more like him as you grow daily.

Daily Do: Is there anyone that needs your help with something you have or can get? Tell your parents about it and do something good for that person.

DAY 81

"THE LORD IS GREAT. HE IS WORTHY OF OUR PRAISE." – PSALM 145:3

Daily Devotional: God is the only being/spirit that is worthy of our praises. No human, gods, or devils are worthy. None of them created heaven and the whole universe. God did.

No one can give life to a human; only God can. He is the only one capable of breathing into a man he made from dust – Making him a living being. Only God can save the soul of a man from sin; he did this by sacrificing his only begotten son, Jesus. And for this reason, he should be praised all over the earth. As the Angels praise him every second, we should praise him too.

Let the words of your lips speak of the praises of God; how awesome and powerful he is; how soon he's going to end all the sufferings of the earth. Speak of his love for humanity, his mercy, and grace that makes him not judge us according to our wrongs. He has been so patient and gentle because he desires for all to be free from sin and come to him.
Praise the Lord! He alone is worthy of our praises!

Daily Do: Sing songs that praise God daily. He delights in your praises.

DAY 82

"WHEN PEOPLE INSULT YOU BECAUSE YOU FOLLOW CHRIST, YOU ARE BLESSED. YOU ARE BLESSED BECAUSE THE SPIRIT OF GOD IS WITH YOU."
– 1 PETER 4:14

Daily Devotional: A follower of Christ will always attract insults from some non-believers. This means that when you stick with Christ and stay away from evil, there will be a rise of people who don't believe in God or what you do. They will mock you because you look foolish in their sight. This happened countless times in history to many old missionaries and evangelists. Jesus Christ who is our Lord and savior was also mocked and insulted for calling himself the son of God. So, if Jesus could handle it, we can too.

Recently, many Christians like you and I face this daily in different countries, and this is why we must continually pray for our fellow brothers and sisters in Christ; that the Lord will preserve them. Now, the Bible says that when people insult you because you follow Christ, you are BLESSED! This is because the spirit of God is with you. The spirit of God is God, and the spirit of God is the breath and the life of God. When you gave your life to Christ, you got his spirit in you. Therefore God lives in you, and that makes you a blessed young man. So, no matter the insult that comes to you from the world as you grow into a man, don't be bothered because God is with you, and that's the best thing that could happen to anyone.

Daily Do: Say this prayer "Dear Lord, help me not to consider the insults men say against me because I follow you; Help me to stay focused on you always, and walk in life like the blessed man that I am" In Jesus name. Amen.

DAY 83

"PRAY FOR ALL PEOPLE. ASK GOD FOR THE THINGS PEOPLE NEED, AND BE THANKFUL TO HIM."
– 1 TIMOTHY 2:1

Daily Devotional: It is your responsibility as a Christian to pray for people, whether you know them or not. It's a command from the Bible. Jesus prayed for the whole world even when we didn't know him or care about him. When he was crucified, he prayed for God to forgive the men that nailed, flogged, and mocked him. That is just so selfless and amazing. Hardly would anyone do that these days because people get angry when wronged by others, and some even seek revenge. But that is not Christ-like. Jesus never sought revenge against his enemies, instead, he prayed for them. He even commanded us in the book of Matthew 5:44 to pray for our enemies. When people hear this, they conclude that it is difficult to do such. Well, it may be difficult, but it's not impossible.

So, pray for people all over the world, ask God for the things they need, which firstly is SALVATION, and then healings, good governance, material things, and so on. And after every prayer, always give thanks that it is done.

Daily Do: As you've learned today, when you pray, remember someone out there who needs your prayers.

DAY 84

"STAND UP. PICK UP YOUR MAT AND WALK."
– JOHN 5:8

Daily Devotional: There was a crippled man at a pool called the "Pool of Bethesda". Many people like this man came there to get healed. But how? You may ask. Well, an angel would come there and stir up the water occasionally, then people would jump into the pool and become healed of their infirmities. So, many got healed every time this happened, sadly this crippled man had been there for many years and never got healed because he couldn't get into the pool, and no one tried to help him either. One day, Jesus came visiting, and he simply told the man "Stand up, pick up your mat and walk". It seemed so strange and impossible because he literally couldn't walk. He thought Jesus would offer to help him into the pool, but no, he just told him to stand up and walk. Why would Jesus say this? Jesus wanted this man to have faith in the power of God. He wanted him to believe that the impossible can become possible. The Bible says For with God all things are possible. So, the man acted in faith, and his legs received strength from God. He suddenly stood up and began to jump in excitement. He couldn't hold in the happiness he felt, and people around him marveled at the great power of God. Now I want you to apply this story to your life. Is there anything you think you can't do? Something you have vowed never to try because you are scared that you might fail. Jesus is telling you today like he told that man at the pool of Bethesda "Stand up, pick your mat and walk" Which means you can do it! The power of God is here to strengthen you to do the impossible. Have faith in God today, and watch what wonders he makes of your life.

Daily Do: Make a decision right now to make a move of faith to do what you thought you couldn't do – good things of course.

85

DAY 85

"DO NOT THINK YOU ARE BETTER THAN YOU ARE."
- ROMANS 12:3

Daily Devotional: The statement the Apostle Paul made to the Roman Christians as seen above refers to the act of arrogance or pride that some of them must have had.

It's the same today as then. Some people are filled with thoughts in their mind that says they are so much better than others around them. They feel they are better than their siblings, friends, classmates, neighbors, etc.

You must not allow such a thought to have a place in your mind. Don't ever think too highly of yourself. It is one thing to believe you can do great things with the help of God, it is another thing to think you are the most handsome and intelligent boy in your school. That's called arrogance. And no one respects arrogant people. Jesus was never arrogant; he was and is the most humble person you could ever meet. So, be like him.

Daily Do: Say this prayer "Lord, I do not want to live an arrogant life; I want to be humble just like you. Help me Lord, make my thoughts and conversations pleasing to you. In Jesus' name" Amen.

DAY 86

"KEEP YOUR HEART WITH ALL DILIGENCE, FOR OUT OF IT SPRINGS THE ISSUES OF LIFE" – PROVERBS 4:23

Daily Devotional: Your heart is like a river that contains everything that flows out of your life; your words, thoughts, and actions are results of what your heart contains; that is why you have to guard your heart diligently. This means that you need to be extra careful of what you allow to get into your heart. Don't listen to or believe negative things you hear about yourself or other people; don't allow hate in your heart. Also, do not speak dirty languages, for they mess up your mind, and before you know it, you begin to think in a dirty way. You are a holy child of God that has been washed clean by the blood of Jesus, so permit nothing from the world to stain you.

Whatever is in a man's heart will eventually control his life. Therefore, let the word of God dwell richly in your heart, and you will find the life of God flowing marvelously in and around you.

Daily Do: Think only about good things, especially the word of God.

DAY 87

"[JESUS] DID NOT COME FOR OTHER PEOPLE TO SERVE HIM. HE CAME TO SERVE OTHERS."
– MATTHEW 20:28

Daily Devotional: Despite the power he possessed, Jesus didn't come for men to serve him; he came to serve men by giving his 'all' for their sake. That includes you and me.

He healed and set many people free from the devil; he still does that today through his chosen vessels. Jesus' ministry was that of service, and that is what he calls us into; to serve.

I have a ministry to fulfill, and you do too. Yes, you do. A ministry is not necessarily a church, it's your act of service for the kingdom of God on the earth. Whatever you do for God to spread the gospel and draw men to him is a ministry. A genuine minister does not do ministry to get something out of it for himself, but for God to be glorified.

Daily Do: Let your life be an act of service to God. He did send you here for a great reason.

DAY 88

"WE WALK BY FAITH, NOT BY SIGHT."
– 2 CORINTHIANS 5:7

Daily Devotional: We are called to a life of faith as children of God. You can't live for God if you don't have faith in him. The fact that you are born again means that you have faith; you got saved by faith, and now you live by faith.

So the Bible defined faith as "...the substance of things hoped for, the evidence of things not seen" Check out the book of Hebrews 11, and you will have a good grasp of what faith is, and how Heroes and Prophets from the Bible walked by it.

Faith is the evidence that God exists, it is the evidence that all God says will come to pass, and that you will be healed and all your needs will be met. The moment you have faith in what you haven't seen yet, that faith is proof that what you believe is true or it's going to happen. I know it sounds weird, but that's what the Bible says. It amazes the angels and every being in heaven and earth when a man lives his life and serves a God he has never even seen. It is a great demonstration of faith. There were a few people in the Bible that had faith that Jesus could heal them, and they got healed. Jesus told them "Your faith has made you whole." For example, read the story of the woman with the issue of blood in the book of Mathew 9:20-22. Additionally, faith is the daily activity of a Christian. The same way a battery powers up a phone, faith powers up a Christian life. And remember "Without faith, no man can please God".

Daily Do: Say this prayer "Help me Lord to keep my faith strong in you as I pray and study your word daily. In Jesus' name" Amen.

DAY 89

"CHRIST'S LOVE IS GREATER THAN ANY PERSON CAN EVER KNOW." – EPHESIANS 3:19

Daily Devotional: The Love of Christ is big, deep, wide, high, (Ephesians 3:18), and altogether the greatest gift that any man could have. When you receive his love, you receive the blessings his sacrifice brings, you receive his life, and you receive his Holy Spirit. The love of Christ is big enough to contain everyone and deep enough to reach even the greatest sinner. His love knows no boundaries; it does not reject anyone, it does not select who is better or nicer; it embraces everyone, and washes away every mud of guilt and sin. His love cleanses our hearts to become like his. It is a beautiful love; it is true love, a love like no other. Truly, his love is the greatest!

Daily Do: There is no love like that of Christ who loved us while we were yet sinners. Think about this daily and give thanks to Jesus for loving you the way he does.

DAY 90

"EVERYONE WHO HEARS MY WORDS AND OBEYS THEM IS LIKE A WISE MAN WHO BUILT HIS HOUSE ON THE ROCK." – MATTHEW 7:24

Daily Devotional: Jesus told a story of a wise man and a foolish man who built houses; the wise man built his house upon a rock, while the foolish man built his upon the sand. When rain fell, winds blew, and floods came, the house built upon the rock stood strong and never fell, but the same weather came upon the house built on sand, and it fell flat like a cookie. Jesus then said that everyone who hears his words and obeys them is just like the wise man that built his house on a rock.

The words of Jesus are the surest and strongest foundation that our lives should be built upon. That way, when challenges and temptation come, we will stand firm and unmovable.

Why do you think the house you live in keeps standing even after many years? Does your house fall flat when heavy rain falls? I believe not. And that is because the foundation it was built on is strong. It's the same for every long-lasting building you see daily. So, your life must stay strong and must never be broken by life or the enemy no matter what. That of course can only be possible by the word of God you hear and obey. Your life is safe on a rock when you trust and walk according to the word of God.

Daily Do: Say this Prayer "Lord I choose to listen and obey your words from now henceforth. So, help me, Lord." Amen.

DAY 91

WHY DO YOU LOOK AT THE SMALL PIECE OF WOOD IN YOUR BROTHER'S EYE AND DO NOT SEE THE BIG PIECE OF WOOD IN YOUR OWN EYE?"
– MATTHEW 7:3

Daily Devotional: Jesus used a really good illustration here to describe how men judge each other. Imagine a man with a piece of wood in his eye (I know that may be difficult), yet he notices the tiny one in his brother's eye. He then says "Look there's a small dirt in your eye, get it out!" while he refuses to see the much bigger one in his eye. That's amusing, but it's exactly what people do, and God frowns at it. How can you have your faults, mistakes, and weaknesses, and then decide to point at the mistakes of another man without dealing with yours first? Jesus called such an act hypocrisy. And back at the time when Jesus was on earth, the religious leaders such as the Pharisees were the hypocrites he constantly referred to. They once tried to stone a woman who committed adultery. She was accused of cheating on her husband with another man, but Jesus said "he who is without sin should cast the first stone" and none of them could; they began to walk away one by one. So, they were sinners, yet they tried to convict or judge another sinner. Jesus then told the woman that her sins had been forgiven, and she should go and sin no more. His mercy upon sinners is incredible!

Daily Do: Is there someone that constantly annoys you? Tell God to help you to be more patient, merciful, and understanding towards the person. So, instead of judging the person, you are becoming a much better son, brother, and friend.

DAY 92

"FOR PEOPLE THIS IS IMPOSSIBLE. BUT FOR GOD ALL THINGS ARE POSSIBLE." – MARK 10:27

Daily Devotional: There are uncountable things that are impossible for men to do, such as casting out devils, healing incurable illnesses, making someone grow a new limb and so many other impossibilities that even science can't figure out. Have you ever imagined how your heart or kidneys were formed? Your whole body was made possible only by God. Scientists can only explain the little they can, and they admit that there are things surely beyond them.

So, when it comes to the problems and challenges in the world today, with man it looks so impossible to solve them, but God says nothing is too difficult for him; with him all things are possible. The man at the corner of the street, who is a drug addict, may look like he would never change, but God says anything is possible; that same man can be redeemed and delivered. He could even become a preacher someday. There are a lot of people with similar stories today.

So, never think anything is impossible for God to do in your life; he is going to make you one of the greatest men on earth if only you would believe him and submit your ways to him.

Daily Do: No matter what you and your family may be going through, know that with God a better day is possible. Stay in faith!

DAY 93

"THE THIEF COMES TO STEAL AND KILL AND DESTROY. BUT I CAME THAT YOU MAY HAVE LIFE AND HAVE IT ABUNDANTLY." – JOHN 10:10

Daily Devotional: The thief referred to here is Satan; he only steals from people, kills them, and destroys their lives. He never does anything good. But Jesus came to save the world so that we may have life in abundance. He gave us eternal life, which is a life that never dies, a life we will spend in heaven; he also gave us a good life on earth, only if we take it.

It is God's will for us as Christians to dominate the world by contributing great things for a better humanity, and yet touching lives with the gospel of truth. He doesn't want you to be poor because you won't be able to achieve much without wealth; he also wants you to be in good health, which is why his healing power is available to you. But seeking wealth and health outside of God is what people do wrong. Never seek anything by pushing God aside. It never turns out well, so get him involved in your journey and let his will prevail in your life.

Daily Do: Say this prayer "Thank you Jesus for the abundant life you have given me. Help me to walk by your will and enjoy this life you have given me" Amen.

DAY 94

"FOR YOU CREATED MY INMOST BEING; YOU KNIT ME TOGETHER IN MY MOTHER'S WOMB. I PRAISE YOU BECAUSE I AM FEARFULLY AND WONDERFULLY MADE; YOUR WORKS ARE WONDERFUL, I KNOW THAT FULL WELL." – PSALM 139:13-14

Daily Devotional: God carefully formed you in your mother's womb; he made your cute face, hands, feet, and every part of your body. When he was done, he smiled and said you looked good – Just as he said when he created the earth. So, you see, God was intentional about you – you are not a mistake. You are a wonderful creature made by the mighty creator – God. He watched over you and cared for you until the day you were born, and he still does the same now, even till you grow old and have grey hairs.

Daily Do: Write this truth boldly in your journal, and think about it daily: "I am fearfully and wonderfully made."

DAY 95

"I CAN DO ALL THINGS THROUGH HIM WHO GIVES ME STRENGTH." – PHILIPPIANS 4:13

Daily Devotional: Have you ever felt weak or not strong enough to do something? Yes, we've all been there.

When the bible says you can do all things through Christ who gives you strength, it isn't saying that you will suddenly have a superpower to lift cars, houses, and mountains. It is simply pointing out that Jesus can strengthen you to handle every challenge you face in life, especially when you lack something you really wish you had. The strength of Jesus helps you to be contented with what you have. That means you are always happy and satisfied with what your parents provide for you, without crying, complaining, and wanting what another kid has.
Be grateful for whatever you have, and if you are not given something you want so much, ask Jesus for it and don't worry or think about it anymore. Trust Jesus always to meet your needs.

Daily Do: A good child is always satisfied with what his parents can afford to get him. Say a big THANK YOU today for everything people do for you. And when things seem tough, say to yourself "I can do all things through Jesus who gives me strength". Now, go make God proud!

DAY 96

IF SOMEONE DOES WRONG TO YOU, FORGIVE THEM. FORGIVE EACH OTHER BECAUSE THE LORD FORGAVE YOU." – COLOSSIANS 3:13

Daily Devotional: Forgiveness is an extremely important aspect of our walk as Christians. You will always be wronged and offended by people, but you choose to forgive them. Although it will feel horrible at first, you are better off when you let go and forgive. Jesus forgave all your sins, so he expects you to do the same with others.

God doesn't want us hating each other, keeping malice, and talking evil of one another. He wants us to show love through forgiveness and kindness. Unforgiveness is like a leach that sucks one's blood; it sucks the life out of you and makes you not fit for God to communicate or relate to.

When you stay angry for too long, it's like a stain on your white garment, you begin to attract house flies instead of butterflies. This means that the spirit of God will not be attracted to you but the spirit of Satan will. The enemy loves the atmosphere of hatred and anger, but God is too holy to hate the human he created, so he forgives. And you have the power to do the same. After all, you are a child of your Father – God.

Daily Do: Is there anyone you feel you need to forgive right now? Do that immediately.

DAY 97

Daily Devotional: As a Christian, you are also part of the army of God; you are one of his soldiers, and he constantly trains you to be strong through your daily experiences. A soldier can not go into the battleground feeling all hungry and weak; he is going to get killed by the enemy. So, as a Christian soldier, you are to feed on the word God daily just as you feed on physical food such as toast and cereal.

The word of God energizes and boosts your faith to fight every battle that confronts you. The word of God injects the mighty power of God inside of you, and you immediately gain supernatural strength to withstand the enemy and his plots against you.

You will find yourself winning all the time when you go into battle with the strength and power of God.

Daily Do: Never give up in the face of challenges. Take up your sword which is the word of God, and fight with the strength that he has placed in you.

DAY 98

BECAUSE OF THE TRUTH, WHICH LIVES IN US AND WILL BE WITH US FOREVER. – 2 JOHN 1:2

Daily Devotional: The truth of God lives in you because you believe in it. This same truth lives in everyone else that believes in the one and only Jesus. Remember he said, "I am the way, the truth, and the life. No man comes to the Father except through me". So Jesus is TRUTH, and anyone who believes and accepts TRUTH will have TRUTH living inside of him. It is that simple.

This truth dwells in us not just for a day, a month, a year, ten years, but forever. And what binds us together as a family in Christ is this truth that we believe in, not our nationality, language, race, personality, etc. What makes us Christians is the fact that we all believe in one truth, which is Jesus.

Daily Do: Say this prayer "Thank you Lord for your truth that dwells in me forever. Help me to spread it to other people too. In Jesus' name" Amen.

DAY 99

WHEN JESUS SPOKE AGAIN TO THE PEOPLE, HE SAID, "I AM THE LIGHT OF THE WORLD. WHOEVER FOLLOWS ME WILL NEVER WALK IN DARKNESS, BUT WILL HAVE THE LIGHT OF LIFE." – JOHN 8:12

Daily Devotional: Jesus is the light of the world; when a man follows light; he sees everything in the dark. So, when you follow Jesus, you are in the light, and darkness will never have a place in your life again.

Aside from being born again, you need to constantly listen to the words he speaks to you. Listen to the people he brings around you, listen to his voice in the scriptures, and live like he is saying them to you directly; that way you will never walk in the dark or be confused about any step or decision you should make as you grow to become a teenager, and then an adult. You will need to make big choices as you grow older, and you will always need the light of the world – Jesus --to guide you on every step.

Additionally, Jesus brings his light to the world through the sacrifice he made by dying on the cross. He brings light to the darkness that the enemy has brought upon the earth by dwelling in the hearts of men who accept him. So, remember this LIGHT DWELLS WITHIN YOU.

Daily Do: Declare this daily "Jesus lives in me so light dwells in me, I am a child of light, and darkness has no place around me"

DAY 100

HE IS NOT HERE, HE IS RISEN!" – MATTHEW 28:6

Daily Devotional: After Jesus died and was buried in a tomb, three days later, his friends Mary Magdalene and another named Mary, went to check where he was buried. Suddenly there was a great earthquake, and the angel of God came down from heaven, rolled away the stone that covered Jesus' tomb, and sat on it. Then the angel said to them "Fear not, for I know you seek for Jesus who was crucified. He is not here, He is risen". The two women were surprised, so they ran with joy in their hearts to tell the disciples of Jesus what the Angel said to them.

Although Jesus died a painful death for no sin committed, he rose after three days, just as he told his disciples he would; though they didn't take him seriously since they barely understood some things he tried to tell them about himself. But when he rose on the third day, it was all so clear, and they all soon believed.

As Christians, the resurrection of Jesus means a lot to us because it proves that we have a savior who is alive in heaven, praying for us. He is God; therefore he couldn't stay dead like an ordinary man. He rose for you and me! And he lives forever more!

Daily Do: Say this prayer "Lord Jesus, I am thankful that you rose from the dead, thank you for living in me, thank you for being who you are. I pledge to spread the good news to the earth, that you are alive forever. So help me Lord" Amen.

DAILY DEVOTIONALS FOR BOYS 8-12

I hope this book allowed you to grow in your relationship with God and with others. Remember following Jesus is not just a one-time thing. It is a lifestyle. Always try to share the love of Christ with your friends, families, and even those who are mean to you. You may think you are just a kid and cannot make a difference, but I promise you...YOU have influence...YOU have an impact...YOU can make a difference for the kingdom of heaven because God chose YOU! Now go live for Him!

Proud of you!
- Randell Holmes Jr

Printed in Great Britain
by Amazon

11959851R00059